Passwords

Passwords

◆

Jean Baudrillard

Translated by Chris Turner

VERSO

London · New York

This edition first published by Verso 2003
© Verso 2003
Translation © Chris Turner 2003
First published as *Mots de passe*
© Pauvert, département des Éditions Fayard 2000
All rights reserved

The moral rights of the author and translator have been asserted

1 3 5 7 9 10 8 6 4 2

Verso
UK: 6 Meard Street, London W1F 0EG
USA: 180 Varick Street, New York, NY 10014–4606
www.versobooks.com

Verso is the imprint of New Left Books

ISBN 1–85984–597–5
ISBN 1–85984–463-4 (pbk)

British Library Cataloguing in Publication Data
A catalogue record for this book is available from the British Library

Library of Congress Cataloging-in-Publication Data
A catalog record for this book is available from the Library of Congress

Typeset in Bembo by YHT Ltd, London
Printed in the UK by Bath Press

CONTENTS

PREFACE

It is paradoxical to form a retrospective overview of an *œuvre* that never sought to be prospective. It is a little like Orpheus turning around too soon to look on Eurydice, and thereby sending her back to the Underworld. It would be acting as though the work pre-existed itself and sensed its end in its very beginnings, as though it were closed, as though it developed in a coherent way, as though it had always existed. I do not see any other way of talking about it, then, than in terms of simulation, rather in the way Borges reconstitutes a lost civilization from the remains of a library. This is to admit that I can scarcely ask myself the question of its sociological verisimilitude — a question I would, indeed, find infinitely difficult to answer. Doubtless one should put oneself in the position of an imaginary traveller who came upon these writings as if they were a lost manuscript and, for want of supporting documents, subsequently strove to reconstitute the society they describe.

INTRODUCTION

Passwords – the expression seems to me to describe quite well a quasi-initiatory way of getting inside things, without, however, drawing up a list. For words are bearers and generators of ideas – perhaps even more than the reverse. As weavers of spells and magic, not only do they transmit those ideas and things, but they themselves metaphorize and metabolize into one another by a kind of spiral evolution. It is in this way that they are 'passers' or vehicles of ideas.

Words are extremely important to me. That they have a life of their own and, hence, are mortal is evident to anyone who does not claim to possess a definitive form of thought, with ambitions to edify. And this is my own case. There is in the temporality of words an almost poetic play of death and rebirth: successive metaphorizations mean that an idea becomes more – and something other – than itself: a 'form of thought'. For language thinks, thinks us and thinks for us at least as much as we think through it. And in it an exchange also takes place: an exchange, which may be symbolic, between words and ideas.

We think we advance by way of ideas – that is doubtless the fantasy of every theorist, every philosopher – but it is also words themselves which generate or regenerate ideas, which act as 'shifters'. At those moments, ideas intersect, intermingle at the level of the word. And the word then serves as an operator – but a non-technical operator – in a catalysis in which language itself is in play. Which makes it at least as important a *stake* in the game as ideas.

Because words pass, then; because they pass away, metamorphose, become 'passers' or vehicles of ideas along unforeseen channels not calculated in advance, the expression 'passwords' seems to me to enable us to reapprehend things, both by crystallizing them and by situating them in an open, panoramic perspective.

THE OBJECT

For me, object will have been the 'password' *par excellence*. I chose that angle from the beginning, because I wanted to break with the problematic of the subject. The question of the object represented the alternative to that problematic, and it has remained the horizon of my thinking. There were also reasons linked to the time we were living through: in the 1960s, the transition from the primacy of production to the primacy of consumption brought objects to the fore. What really interested me, however, was not so much the manufactured object in itself, but how objects spoke to each other – the system of signs and the syntax they developed. And, particularly, the fact that they referred to a world less real than the apparent omnipotence of consumption and profit might have led us to believe. As I saw it, in that world of signs, they very quickly broke away from their use-value to enter into play and correspondence with one another.

Behind this semiological formalism there was no doubt a memory of Sartre's *Nausea* and that famous root which is an obsessive object, a poisonous substance . . . It seemed to me that the object was almost fired with passion, or at least that it could have a life of its own; that it could leave behind the passivity of its use to acquire a kind of autonomy, and perhaps even a capacity to avenge itself on a subject over-sure of controlling it. Objects have always been regarded as an inert, dumb world, which is ours to do with as we will, on the grounds that we produced it. But, for me, that world had something to say which exceeded its use. It was part of the realm of the sign, where nothing happens so simply, because the sign always effaces the thing. So the object designated the real world, but also its absence – and, in particular, the absence of the subject.

It was the exploration of that fauna and flora of objects that interested me. In that exploration I used all the disciplines current at the time: psychoanalysis, the Marxist analysis of production and, especially, following the example of Barthes, linguistic analysis. But the advantage of studying the object was that it required you to move across these disciplines; it forced a cross-disciplinarity on you. The fact was that the object was reducible to no particular discipline and, rendering them all enigmatic, helped to throw into question their very postulates – including those of semiology in so far as the sign-object, within which there is an interplay between many types of values, is much more ambiguous than the linguistic sign.

Whatever the real interest of these different approaches, what excited me, and still does, is the way the object slips away, absents itself – all that it retains of the *Unheimlich*, the 'uncanny'. The exchange, of which it is the medium, remains unconsummated. The object is, admittedly, med-

4

iatory, but at the same time, because it is immediate, immanent, it shatters that mediation. It is on both sides of the line, and it both gratifies and disappoints. So, it has its origin perhaps in that 'accursed share' Bataille speaks of, which will never be resolved or redeemed. There is no Redemption of the object. Somewhere there is a 'remainder', which the subject cannot lay hold of, which he believes he can overcome by profusion, by accumulation, and which in the end merely puts more and more obstacles in the way of relating. In a first phase, one communicates through objects, then proliferation blocks that communication. The object has a dramatic role. It is a fully fledged actor in that it confounds any mere functionality. And it is in that respect that it interests me.

VALUE

Clearly, value is intimately linked to the object, but what I am concerned with here is more limited and relates to use-value and exchange-value, those foundations of production and the market. From the outset, use-value and exchange-value – and the dialectic established between the two – appeared to me to be a rational construction that postulates the possibility of balancing out value, of finding a general equivalent for it which is capable of exhausting meanings and accounting for an exchange. It was at this point that anthropology came in, to undermine these notions and shatter the ideology of the market – that is to say, the market as ideology, and not simply as reality. Anthropology gives us access to societies and cultures in which the notion of value as we understand it is virtually non-existent, in which things are never exchanged directly one for another, but always through the mediating agency of a transcendence, an abstraction.

Alongside commodity value there exist moral or aesthetic values which operate, for their part, in terms of a set opposition between good and bad, between the beautiful and the ugly ... It seemed to me, however, that there was a possibility for things to circulate differently, and other cultures did indeed offer the image of a form of organization in which the transcendence of value, and with it the transcendence of power, was not established, since it is on the manipulation of values that that transcendence is constituted. It was a question of attempting to strip the object – but not just the object – of its status as commodity, to restore to it an immediacy, a brute reality which would not have a price put on it. Either a thing is 'worthless', or it is 'priceless'; in either case we are dealing with what cannot be evaluated, in the strongest sense of the term. From that point on, the exchange that can be effected operates on foundations that are no longer of the order of the contract – as in the usual system of value – but of the pact. There is a profound difference between the contract, which is an abstract convention between two terms or individuals, and the pact, which is a dual, collusive relation. We might see an image of this in certain modalities of poetic language in which exchanges between words – with the intensity of pleasure they afford – are made outside the sphere of their mere decipherment, before or beyond their operation in terms of 'meaning value'. It is the same for objects and individuals. From this standpoint, there is a possibility of short-circuiting the system of value and the sphere of ascendancy it establishes. It is on the basis of meaning that one will be master of language, master of communication (even if the speech act and its modalities come into play in this mastery of discourse); it is on the basis of market value that one will have mastery of the market. And it is on the distinction between the values of good and evil that moral ascendancy will be established . . . All powers are subsequently built on this. It is perhaps utopian to claim to pass beyond value, but it is an operative utopia, an attempt to conceive a more radical functioning of things.

The fact remains that the study of value is complex: whereas commodity value can be apprehended, sign value is fleeting and fluid – at a particular point it gives out and is frittered into 'show'. When everything eventually gives way to artifice, are we still in a world of value, or in its simulation?

Perhaps we are always in a dual morality . . . There might be said to be a moral sphere, that of commodity exchange, and an immoral sphere, that of play or gaming, where all that counts is the event of the game itself and the advent of shared rules. Sharing rules is something quite different from referring to a common general equivalent: to be able to play, one has to be totally involved. And this creates a more dramatic type of relation between the partners than commodity exchange. In such a relation, individuals are not abstract beings who can be substituted one for another: each has a singular position with regard to stakes of victory or defeat, life or death. Even in its most banal forms, the mode of entry into what is at stake that gaming forces upon us is different from that imposed by exchange – a word which is, indeed, so ambiguous that I have begun, rather, to talk about impossible exchange.

SYMBOLIC EXCHANGE

Symbolic exchange is the strategic site where all the modalities of value flow together towards what I would term a blind zone, in which everything is called into question again. The symbolic here does not have the usual sense of 'imaginary', nor the sense given to it by Lacan. It is symbolic exchange as anthropology understands it. Whereas value always has a unidirectional sense, whereas it passes from one point to another according to a system of equivalence, in symbolic exchange the terms are reversible. The point for me in using this concept was to take the opposite stance from commodity exchange and, in that way, make a political critique of our society in the name of something that might perhaps be dubbed utopian, but that has been a living concept in many other cultures.

Reversibility is simultaneously the reversibility of life and death, of good and evil, and of all that we have organized in terms of alternative values. In the symbolic universe, life and death are exchanged. And, since there are no separate terms but, rather, reversibility, the idea of value is cast into question, requiring as it does distinctly opposed terms between which a dialectic can then be established. Now, there is no dialectic in the symbolic. Where death and life are concerned, there is in our system of values no reversibility: what is positive is on the side of life, what is negative is on the side of death; death is the end of life, its opposite, whereas in the symbolic universe the terms are, strictly speaking, exchanged.

This applies in all fields, and hence also in that of the exchange of goods: in potlatch a certain type of circulation of goods operates, exonerated from the idea of value, a type of circulation which includes prodigality and the squandering of things, but must never stop. Exchange must never have an end, it must always increase in intensity, possibly continuing until death. Gaming might also be said to be of the order of this form of exchange, in so far as money no longer has any fixed value within that sphere, since it is always put back into circulation according to the symbolic rule – which is clearly not the moral law. In this symbolic rule, money won must in no circumstances become commodity value again; it must be put back into play within the game itself.

We may also extend this symbolic exchange to a broader level: the level of forms. So the animal form, the human form, the divine form are exchanged according to a rule of metamorphoses in which each ceases to be confined to its definition, with the human opposed to the inhuman, etc. There is a symbolic circulation of things in which none has a separate individuality, in which all operate in a kind of universal collusiveness of inseparable forms. It is the same with the body, which does not have any 'individual' status either: it is a kind of sacrificial substitute that is not opposed to some other substance such as the soul or any other spiritual value. In those cultures where the body is continually brought into play in ritual, it is not the symbol of life and the question is not that of its health, survival or integrity. Whereas we have an individualized view of the body, linked to notions of possession and mastery, there it is subject to a constant reversibility. It is a substance which can move through other – animal, mineral or vegetable – forms.

And indeed, isn't everything always decided at the level of a symbolic exchange – that is to say, at a level that goes far beyond the rational commerce of things or bodies as we practise it today? In fact, paradoxical as it may seem, I would be quite willing to believe that there has never been any economy in the rational scientific sense in which we understand it, that symbolic exchange has always been at the radical base of things, and that it is on that level that things are decided.

We may choose to regard this symbolic exchange as something we have lost, to interest ourselves in potlatch in primitive societies and treat it anthropologically, taking the view that, so far as we are concerned, we are totally in market societies, in societies governed by value ... But is this so certain? Perhaps we are still in an immense potlatch. We delimit areas in which kinds of economic, anatomical and sexual rationalities seem to come together, but the fundamental form, the radical form, is still that of challenge, of one-upmanship, of potlatch – and hence of the negation, the sacrifice of value. So we might be said to be living still in a sacrificial mode, without wishing to acknowledge it. Without being able to either because, without the rituals, without the myths, we no longer have the means to do so.

There is no point being nostalgic for it: we have established another form of organization that has created an irreversible, linear system where there was previously a circular form, a circuit, reversibility. We live, then we die, and that is truly the end.

SEDUCTION

For me, the universe of seduction was what stands out radically against the universe of production. It was no longer a question of bringing things forward, of manufacturing them, of producing them for a world of value, but of seducing them – that is to say, of diverting them from that value, and hence from their identity, their reality, to destine them for the play of appearances, for their symbolic exchange. That symbolic exchange originally had the economic world as its target: goods – as in potlatch – and then the symbolic exchange of death. Then came sexuality, which slightly narrowed the field. As I understand the term, seduction involves everything, not simply the exchange between the sexes. Admittedly, by its difference, each sex seeks out and finds its identity by confronting the other in a form both of rivalry and of connivance, positivizing sexuality as function and as *jouissance*. But seduction for me was, first, that reversible form in which both physiological sexes played out their identity, put themselves in play. What interested me was a kind of becoming-masculine of the feminine and becoming-feminine of the masculine, against the prejudiced view that the masculine in itself is sexual identity. I understood the feminine as that which contradicts the masculine/

feminine opposition, the value opposition between the two sexes. The feminine was that which transversalized these notions and, in a manner of speaking, abolished sexual identity. I have to say that this produced some misunderstandings with the feminists. Particularly as, from this standpoint, what was at issue was no longer sexual liberation, which seemed to me in the end quite a naive project since it was based on value, on sexual identity . . .

Seduction is a more fatal game, and a more dangerous one too, which is in no way exclusive of pleasure, but is something different from *jouissance*. Seduction is a challenge, a form which tends always to unsettle someone in their identity and the meaning they can have for themselves. In seduction they find the possibility of a radical otherness. Seduction seemed to me to cover all the forms that elude a system of accumulation, of production. Now, sexual liberation – which was the great cause of that period, just like the liberation of the workers – was still conceived within the productivist schema. It was a matter of liberating energy – the archetypal model of which was material energy – a model in absolute contradiction to the great game of seduction which, for its part, is not accumulative in nature.

Seduction is not so much a play on desire as a playing with desire. It does not deny it, nor is it its opposite, but it sets it in play.

Appearances belong to the sphere of seduction, far beyond physical appearances. It is the sphere in which putting beings into play is a kind of ethic, a sphere of flexible, reversible forms where neither sex is assured of its foundation nor, above all, of its superiority. I had, then, played the feminine card, where, in symbolic exchange, I had previously played that of death. It was a kind of password – of pass-reality, if I may put it that way: a sort of index of the reversibility of life and death. The *femina* was, thus, the reversibility of the masculine and the feminine.

Yet I should make one thing clear: the term 'seduction' has been used everywhere and anywhere in a whole string of senses, such as 'power seduces the masses', the 'seduction of the media' or the 'great seducers' … I did not mean the term at that level which is, after all, extremely vulgar. It is true that it seemed to me that historically, women had a privileged position in the field of seduction. But some have taken the view that to link women and seduction was to consign them to the realm of appearances – and hence to frivolity. This is a total misunderstanding: the seduction I was referring to is really the symbolic mastery of forms, whereas the other is merely the material mastery of power by way of a stratagem.

The original crime is seduction. And our attempts to positivize the world, to give it a unilateral meaning, like the whole immense undertaking of production, are no doubt aimed at abolishing this ultimately dangerous, evil terrain of seduction.

For this world of forms — seduction, challenge, reversibility — is the more powerful one. The other, the world of production, has power; but potency, for its part, lies with seduction. I do not think that it is primary in terms of cause and effect, in terms of succession, but it is more potent, in the more or less long term, than all the systems of production — of wealth, meaning or *jouissance* … And all the types of production are perhaps subordinate to it.

THE OBSCENE

'Scene' and 'obscene' do not, of course, have the same etymology, but it is tempting to connect the two. For as soon as there is a scene or a stage, there is gaze and distance, play and otherness. The spectacle is bound up with the scene. On the other hand, when we are in obscenity, there is no longer any scene or stage, any play, and the distance of the gaze is abolished. Let us take the pornographic sphere: it is clear that in pornography the body is, in its entirety, *realized*. Perhaps the definition of obscenity might be, then, the becoming-real, the becoming-absolutely-real, of something which until then was treated metaphorically, or had a metaphorical dimension. Sexuality – and seduction too – always has a metaphorical dimension. In obscenity, the body, the sex organs, the sex act are brutally no longer '*mis en scène*', but immediately proffered for view or, in other words, for devouring; they are absorbed and resorbed at one and the same time. It is a total 'acting out' of things that ought to be subject to a dramaturgy, a scene, a play between partners. Here there is no play, no dialectic or separation, but a total collusion of the elements.

What is true of bodies is true of the media coverage of an event, of 'information'. When things become too real, when they are immediately given and realized, when we are in the short circuit which means that these things are brought closer and closer together, we are in obscenity. From this standpoint, Régis Debray made an interesting critique of the society of the spectacle: according to him, we are no longer in a society which distances us from things, in which we could be said to be alienated by our separation from them ... Our curse is that we are brought up ultra-close against them, that everything is immediately realized, both things and ourselves. And this too-real world is obscene.

In such a world, what we have is not communication, but contamination of a viral type; everything spreads from one person to another in an immediate fashion. The term 'promiscuity' describes the same process: things are there immediately, without distance and without charm. And without genuine pleasure.

These are the two extremes: obscenity and seduction, as is shown by art, which is one of the terrains of seduction. On the one hand, there is art, which is capable of inventing a scene other than the real, another set of rules; on the other, there is realist art, which has fallen into a kind of obscenity by becoming descriptive, objective or the pure reflection of the decomposition – the fractalization – of the world.

There are uppings of the stakes in obscenity: it may already be crudely obscene to present the naked body; to present it emaciated, flayed and skeletal is even more so. It is clear today that the entire critical problematic of the media revolves around this threshold of tolerance for the excess of obscenity. If everything has to be said, then everything will be ... But objective truth is obscene. The fact remains that when we are told all the details of Bill Clinton's sexual activities, the obscenity is so laughable that we wonder whether there isn't an ironic dimension to it. This ironic turnabout might perhaps be the last avatar of seduction in a world in perdition, in total obscenity: all the same, deep down, we cannot quite manage to believe this. Obscenity – that is to say, the total visibility of things – is unbearable to the point where we have to apply an ironic strategy to survive. Otherwise this particular transparency would be totally lethal.

We find ourselves, then, between good and evil, in an irresolvable antagonism in which – at the risk of being Manichaean, and contradicting the whole of our humanism – there is no possible reconciliation. We have to accept these rules of the game, which, though they are no consolation, seem to me more clear-sighted than thinking we shall one day unify the world and restore the hypothetical realm of good. It is precisely when we try to achieve such a total good that evil surfaces. Paradoxical as it may seem, is it not through human rights – and at the planetary level – that the worst discrimination occurs? So, the pursuit of good has perverse effects, and those perverse effects are always on the side of evil. But to speak of evil is not to condemn: in a sense, evil is that which is fated – and fate can be unfortunate or fortunate.

THE TRANSPARENCY OF EVIL

All 'transparency' immediately raises the question of its opposite, secrecy. This is an alternative that is in no way of the order of morality, of good and evil: there is what is secret and what is generally known, which is a different sort of distinction. Certain things will never be put on open view; they are shared in secrecy as part of a type of exchange that is different from the one that involves visibility. When everything tends towards the visible, as is the case in our world, what becomes of the things that were once kept secret? They become occult, clandestine, maleficent: what was merely secret – or, in other words, given to be exchanged in secrecy – becomes evil and must be abolished, exterminated. But these things cannot be destroyed: in a certain sense, secrecy is indestructible. It will then be diabolized, and come out through the very instruments used to eliminate it. Its energy is that of evil, the energy that comes from the non-unification of things – good being defined as the unification of things in a totalized world.

From this point on, everything based on duality, on the dissociation of things, on negativity, on death, is regarded as evil. Our society works, then, to ensure that all is to the good, that there is a technology to meet every need. In this sense, all technology is on the side of good or, in other words, of the fulfilment of general desire in a unified state of things.

We are today in what I would call a 'Moebius-strip' system. If we were in a face-to-face, confrontational system, strategies could be clear, based on a linearity of causes and effects. Whether one used good or evil, it would be used as part of a plan, and Machiavellianism would not lie outside rationality. But we are in a completely random universe in which causes and effects are piled one upon the other according to this Moebius-strip model, and no one can know where the effects of the effects will end.

An example of a perverse effect can be seen in the struggle against the corruption prevalent in business, or in the funding of political parties. It is clear that this must be condemned. And the judges condemn it. And we tell ourselves this represents a clean-up, a cleansing in the good sense of the term. But this clean-up also necessarily has secondary effects. The Clinton affair is of the same order. By managing to condemn a perversion of justice that verges on the betrayal of a solemn oath, the judge is contributing to building the image of a 'clean' America. And one, therefore, which benefits from an enhanced moral power to exploit the rest of the world (even if it does so democratically).

It is only superficially that we can read the action of the judges as opposed conflictually to the political class. In a way, they are, rather, the regenerators of its legitimacy – even though the problem of its corruption is far from being resolved.

And is it so certain that corruption must be eradicated at all costs? We tell ourselves, of course, that it would be far preferable to use the money that goes on the fabulous commissions paid for funding arms deals, or even on arms production, to reduce world poverty. But that is to jump to a hasty conclusion. Since there is no question of the money being taken out of the commodity circuit, it 'could' be redirected into a generalized concreting-over of the land. Given this state of affairs, paradoxical as the question may seem, is it preferable from the point of view of 'good' or 'evil', to continue to manufacture – and, indeed, to sell – weapons, a certain number of which will never be used, or to have a country disappear beneath a blanket of concrete? The answer to this question is of less importance than the realization that there is no fixed point from which we can determine what is totally good or totally evil.

This, of course, is a profoundly disastrous – and entirely uncomfortable – situation for the rational mind. The fact remains that, in the same way as Nietzsche spoke of the vital illusion of appearances, we might speak of a vital function of corruption in society. But, since the principle of corruption is illegitimate, it cannot be made official, and hence can operate only in secret. This is a clearly cynical, morally inadmissible viewpoint, but it is also a kind of fatal strategy – which is not, indeed, anyone's particular prerogative, and affords no exclusive benefits. Evil might be said to be reintroduced by this route. Evil functions because it is from it that energy comes. And to fight it – which is necessary – leads simultaneously to reactivating it.

We may mention here what Mandeville said when he asserted that a society operates on the basis of its vices, or at least on the basis of its disequilibria. Not on its positive qualities, but on its negative qualities. If we accept this cynicism, we can understand that politics should be – also – the inclusion of evil, of disorder, in the ideal order of things. We should not, then, deny evil, but play on it, play fast and loose with it, play it false.

This title – 'the transparency of evil' – is not entirely apposite ... We should speak, rather, of the transpiring, the 'showing-through' [*transparition*] of Evil which, whatever we do, 'shows through' or transpires through everything that strives to ward it off. Moreover, it might be said to be transparency itself that is the Evil – the loss of all secrecy. Just as, in the 'perfect crime', it is the perfection itself that is criminal.

THE VIRTUAL

In its current sense, the virtual stands opposed to the real, but its sudden emergence, through the new technologies, gives us the sense that it now marks the vanishing or end of the real. I have already said that, as I see it, to bring a real world into being is in itself to produce that world, and the real has only ever been a form of simulation. We may, admittedly, cause a reality-effect, a truth-effect or an objectivity-effect to exist, but, in itself, the real does not exist. The virtual, then, is merely a hyperbolic instance of this tendency to pass from the symbolic to the real – which is its degree zero. In this sense, the virtual coincides with the notion of hyperreality. Virtual reality, the reality that might be said to be perfectly homogenized, digitized and 'operationalized', substitutes for the other because it is perfect, verifiable and non-contradictory. So, because it is more 'complete', it is more real than what we have established as simulacrum.

The fact remains that this expression, 'virtual reality', is positively an oxymoron. We no longer have the good old philosophical sense of the term, where the virtual was what was destined to become actual, or where a dialectic was established between these two notions. The virtual now is what takes the place of the real; it is the final solution of the real in so far as it both accomplishes the world in its definitive reality and marks its dissolution.

At this point, it is the virtual which thinks us: no need now for a subject of thought, a subject of action; everything happens by techno-logical mediation. But is the virtual that which puts an end, once and for all, to a world of the real and of play, or is it part of an experimentation with which we are playing? Are we not playing out the comedy of the virtual to ourselves, with a hint of irony, as in the comedy of power? In the end, isn't this immense installation of virtuality, this performance in the artistic sense, a new stage on which operators have replaced actors? If this were the case, there would be no need to attach any more belief to it than to any other ideological formation. This is rather a reassuring hypothesis: in the end, this whole issue would not seem to be very serious, and the extermination of reality would be anything but firmly established.

But if our world is indeed inventing a virtual double for itself, we have to see this as the fulfilment of a trend that began long ago. Reality, as we know, has not always existed. We have talked about it only since there has been a rationality to express it, parameters enabling us to represent it by coded and decodable signs.

In the virtual, we are no longer dealing with value; we are merely dealing with a turning-into-data, a turning-into-calculations, a general-ized computation in which reality-effects disappear. The virtual might be said to be truly the reality-horizon, just as we talk about the event-horizon in physics. But it is also possible to think that all this is merely a roundabout route towards an as yet indiscernible aim.

There is a positive fascination today with the virtual and all its technologies. If it genuinely is a mode of disappearance, this would be an – obscure, but deliberate – choice on the part of the species itself: the decision to clone itself, lock, stock and barrel, in another universe; to disappear as the human race, properly speaking, in order to perpetuate itself in an artificial species that would have much more efficient, much more operational attributes. Is this what is at issue?

What comes to mind here is Borges's fable of the people ostracized and pushed to the other side of the mirror, who are now merely the reflection of the emperor who subjugated them.[1] We might see the great system of the virtual like this, and all the rest as merely kinds of clones, forms of rejection and abjection. But in the fable these people begin to look less and less like their dominator, and one day they come back through the mirror. This time, says Borges, they will not be defeated. Can we suppose a catastrophe of this kind, and at the same time this kind of revolution to

---

1. J.L. Borges, 'Fauna of Mirrors', in *The Book of Imaginary Beings* (Harmondsworth: Penguin, 1974), pp. 67–8 [Trans.].

the third power? Personally, I am more inclined to imagine such a hypertrophy of the virtual that we would arrive at a form of implosion. What would take its place? It is difficult to say because, beyond the virtual, I see nothing but what Freud called 'nirvana', an exchange of molecular substance and nothing more. All that would remain would be a perfect wave system, which would join up with the system of particles in a purely physical universe that no longer had anything human, moral, or – obviously – metaphysical about it. In this way, we would have returned to a material stage, with a senseless circulation of elements . . .

Leaving science fiction behind, we can only note, after all, the peculiar irony there is in the fact that these technologies, which we associate with inhumanity and annihilation, will in the end, perhaps, be what frees us from the world of value, the world of judgement. All this heavy moral, philosophical culture, which modern radical thought has done its meta-physical utmost to liquidate after a back-breaking struggle, technology expels pragmatically and radically with the virtual.

At the stage we are at, we do not know whether technology, having reached a point of extreme sophistication, will liberate us from tech-nology itself – the optimistic viewpoint – or whether in fact we are heading for catastrophe. Even though catastrophes, in the dramaturgical sense of the term – that is to say, endings – may, depending on the protagonists, assume happy or unhappy forms.

RANDOMNESS

The random – to which I would add the fractal and the catastrophic – is part of those modern theories which take account of the unforeseeable effects of things or, at the very least, of a certain dissemination of effects and causes such that reference points disappear. We are in a random world, a world in which there is no longer a subject and an object distributed harmoniously within the register of knowledge. As for random phenomena, they are not simply in things, in material bodies: we, too, are part of the molecular microcosm by our very thought – and that is what creates the radical uncertainty of the world. If we were dealing with a random matter, with random physical effects, but with a thinking which was, for its part, homogeneous and unidirectional, then there would still be a solid dialectic between subject and object, but we have fallen now into a random thinking which no longer allows us to do any more than propound hypotheses, a thinking which can no longer lay claim to truth. This is already the case in the subatomic sciences, as we know. But I believe it is also the case with our thinking on, and current analysis of, society and the political sphere . . . All we can do now is meet random processes halfway, by means of a thinking that is itself random, which is a quite different exercise from the classic discursive thought that founded traditional philosophy. This new way of proceeding is not without its dangers. What can we refer to as 'events' when things unfold in a predominantly chaotic manner, with minimal, infinitesimal causes or initial conditions, and prodigious effects on a world scale? In this sense the phenomenon of globalization is in itself random and chaotic, to the point where no one can control it or claim to subject it to a strategy.

The fractal is also at the centre of our world. I shall not talk about Mandelbrot's theories, with which I am not sufficiently familiar, but this indefinite reproduction of a single micro-form, of a single formula, calls to mind our situation, in so far as we are infinitesimal particles in which all the information concentrated in each one merely now proliferates, repeating an identical formula.

The mass phenomenon, as identified in sociology, was already a fractal phenomenon, a virtual phenomenon, a viral phenomenon. All these dimensions, which have had their historical phase of emergence, are also found in the physics of mass. Might it be the case that we are left now with fractal individuals – that is to say, individuals not divided (something which assured them still of an – albeit problematical – integrity), but disseminated, multiplied to infinity? Culturally, individuals are already cloned; they do not need to be cloned biologically, genetically. Perhaps they will be, but in any event they are already cloned mentally and culturally: this development is quite clearly perceptible.

In the face of these chaotic and catastrophic forms, and their processes of exponentiality, we can see that the human macrocosm, which we imagined we would universalize through a mastery of the world by rationality, has become a bubble inside a completely uncontrollable microcosm that is of a micro-physical, random order. The rule is henceforth the molecular, the random. As for the real, for meaning and for truth, they are the exceptions – that is to say, a mystery. How can this truth-effect and this reality-effect have been born somewhere, at some tiny point in the universe, and have endured for however short a time – even if they are now dying out?

CHAOS

Chaos is not radically opposed to rationality. Rationality we have more or less mastered, but even the sciences are reaching their outer limits: at a certain point, we come up against the object barrier, and physical laws reverse themselves or no longer operate. However, we have not yet left behind the utopian goal of increasingly sophisticated knowledge, even though that radical illusion is not internal to science. For my part, I would be quite happy to put forward an almost Manichaean hypothesis: in the last instance, we might be said to be faced not with an appropriation of the object of the world by the subject, but with a duel between subject and object. And, as regards the outcome, all bets are still on . . . One very much has the impression that there is a kind of turnabout, of revenge, almost of vengeance, on the part of the allegedly passive object, which allowed itself to be discovered and analysed, but has suddenly become a 'strange attractor' and, in a manner of speaking, an opponent. Here, something akin to a fatal antagonism is being played out, of the order of that between Eros and Thanatos, in a kind of metaphysical clash.

Today, our sciences confess to the strategic disappearance of the object on the Virtual Display Unit: the object is henceforth beyond our grasp.

As it happens, I find this very ironic: the rules of the game are chan-
ging, but it is no longer we who set them. That is the destiny of a culture:
our own. Other cultures, other metaphysics, are doubtless not so badly
undermined by this development because they did not have the ambition,
expectation or phantasm of possessing the world, of analysing it in order
to control it. But since we claimed to control the totality of postulates, it
is clearly *our* system that is heading for catastrophe.

THE END

With this word, it is the question of time that is posed, the question of its linearity, of this – perhaps conventional – representation we have of it as past, present and future, with an origin and an end. There is an origin–end couple in the same way as there are causes and effects, subject and object: all these reassuring things. But, from now on, we are in a kind of process of limitlessness in which the end can no longer be located. I have spoken, in this connection, of a 'final solution', in the sense of an extermination.

But the end is also the finality or purpose of something, that which gives it a meaning. And when you are in processes developing in a chain reaction, which, beyond a certain critical mass, become exponential, they no longer have any finality or meaning. Canetti notes this in relation to history: we have, he says, passed beyond the true and the false, beyond good and evil, and there is no way back. On this view, there is a kind of point of irreversibility beyond which things lose their end. When something comes to an end, this means it really took place; whereas if there no longer is any end, we enter interminable history, interminable crisis; we enter upon series of interminable processes. We know these;

they are already here: we simply have to look at the interminable, excessive development of material production.

In this system, there is no longer any coming to a term. On the occasion of our passing the year 2000, I wanted to see if we still had this sense of a term falling due, or if we were in a mere countdown. The countdown is not the end; it is the extenuation of something, the exhaustion of a process, which does not, for all that, come to an end, but which becomes interminable. We stand, then, before a paradoxical alternative: either we shall never reach the end, or we are already beyond it. Personally, I told myself there would be no 'passing' to the year 2000 because it had taken place long ago; that what was involved here was merely a kind of somersaulting of temporality. So, unable to locate an end, we strive desperately to pin down a beginning. Our current compulsion to seek out origins is testament to this: in the anthropological and palaeontological fields we see limits being pushed back in time, into a past that is also interminable.

My hypothesis is that we have already passed the point of irreversibility; that we are already in an exponential, unlimited form in which everything develops in the void, to infinity, without any possibility of reapprehending it in a human dimension; in which we are losing the memory of the past, the projection of the future and the possibility of integrating that future into a present action. We might be said already to be in an abstract, disembodied state where things continue by mere inertia and become simulacra of themselves, without our being able to put an end to them. They are now merely an artificial synthesis, a prosthesis. Admittedly, this assures them of an existence and a kind of immortality and eternity – that of the clone, of a clone universe. The problem raised by history is not that it might have come to an end, as Fukuyama says, but rather that it will have no end – and hence no longer any finality, any purpose.

I have dealt with this question of the end in terms of illusion. We always harbour the illusion that something will have an end-point, that it will then take on a meaning, and will allow us retrospectively to restore its origin and, with this beginning and this end, the play of cause and effect will become possible . . .

The absence of end gives us the sense that all the information we receive is merely something predigested and rehashed, that everything was already there, that we are faced with a melodramatic mishmash of events, not knowing whether they really took place or not, whether they aren't substitutes for others – which is quite different from an event that could not but take place, the fated event, which really marks the end but possesses the status of event by dint of its very fatedness.

The fact of having extradited death – or, at the very least, of constantly attempting to – shows up in the endless efforts made to delay the onset of things: to stop growing old, to eliminate alternatives, to have advance control even over birth, drawing on all the possibilities of genetics.

Because all these possibilities are technologically plausible, technology has replaced the determination which means that at a given moment two things are mutually exclusive, that they separate and will have a different destiny, but also the infinite possibility of doing everything one thing after the other. We have here, if not two opposite metaphysics (in so far as technology is not of a metaphysical order), at least a crucial issue where freedom is concerned.

But if there is no longer any end or finitude, if the subject is immortal, then he no longer knows who he is. And it is this immortality that is the ultimate phantasm of our technologies.

THE PERFECT CRIME

The perfect crime would be the elimination of the real world. But what concerns me, rather, is the elimination of the original illusion, the fateful illusion of the world. We might agree that the world itself is a perfect crime: it has in itself no motive, no equivalent, no alleged perpetrator. So we may imagine that, from the very beginning, we are already in a criminal enterprise.

But in the perfect crime, it is the perfection that is criminal. To perfect the world is to finish it, to fulfil it – and hence to find a final solution for it. I have in mind the parable of the Tibetan monks who, for centuries, have been deciphering all the names of God, the nine billion names of God.[2] One day they call in the people from IBM, who turn up with their computers, and within a month they have finished the whole job. Now the monks' prophecy said that once this listing of the names of God was finished, the world would come to an end. Obviously the IBM people do

---

2. Arthur C. Clarke, 'The Nine Billion Names of God', in *Of Time and Stars* (London: Penguin, 1992), pp. 17–23 [Trans.].

not believe this but, as they are coming back down the mountain, with their inventory completed, they see the stars in the sky extinguished one by one. This is a very fine parable of the extermination of the world by its ultimate verification, which perfects it with calculations, with truth.

Faced with a world that is illusion, all the great cultures have striven to manage the illusion by illusion – to treat evil with evil, so to speak. We alone seek to reduce the illusion with truth – which is the most fantastical of illusions. But this ultimate truth, this final solution, is the equivalent of extermination. What is at issue in the perfect crime perpetrated on the world, on time, on the body, is this kind of dissolution by the objective verification of things, by identification. This is equivalent to eliminating death once again, as I have already said. For what is involved here is no longer death, but extermination. Literally, to *exterminate* means to deprive something of its own end, to deprive it of its term. It is to eliminate duality, the antagonism of life and death, to reduce everything to a kind of single principle – we might say a *pensée unique* – of the world, which could be said to express itself in all our technologies, particularly today our virtual technologies.

So, it is both a crime against the real world, which becomes a useless function, but, more deeply, more radically, it is a crime perpetrated against the illusion of the world, that is to say, against its radical uncertainty, its duality, its antagonism – everything which underlies the existence of destiny, conflict and death. So, by eliminating every negative principle, we might be said to end up with a world that is unified, homogenized, totally *verified*, as it were, and hence, as I see it, exterminated. Extermination might be said, from this point on, to be our new mode of disappearance, the one we have substituted for death.

Such is the story of the perfect crime, which shows itself in the whole current 'operationality' of the world, in our ways of *realizing* those things that are dreams, phantasms, utopias, transcribing them digitally, turning them into information, which is the work of the virtual in its most widely accepted sense. This is the crime: we attain a perfection in the sense of a total accomplishment, and that totalization is an end. There is no longer any destination elsewhere, nor even any 'elsewhere'. The perfect crime destroys otherness, the other. It is the reign of the same. The world is identified with itself, identical to itself, by exclusion of any principle of otherness.

Today, what underlies the notion of 'individual' is not the philosophical subject or the critical subject of history, but a perfectly operational molecule that is left to its own devices and doomed to be answerable for itself alone. Having no destiny, it will have merely a precoded development and it will reproduce, self-identically, to infinity. This 'cloning', in the most widely accepted sense, is part of the perfect crime.

DESTINY

Where destiny is concerned, I would be inclined to use an image borrowed from the geographical realm, namely that of the famous 'continental divide' from which, in the USA, some waters run off towards the Pacific and others towards the Atlantic. As a result of that divide, two elements separate irreversibly at a given point, it seems, and will never meet up again. The divide occurs once and for all. We may say the same of birth, which is a definitive separation. Something assumes the form of existence, something else does not – and what is not born will at the same time become the other, and will remain so.

Destiny might be said, then, to be a form of definitive, irreversible separation. But a kind of reversibility means that the things that are separated will remain in collusion. Subatomic particle physics speaks of both the *separability* and the *inseparability* of particles. Wherever they go, and even though they diverge definitively, each particle remains bound, connected to its antiparticle. I cannot push this analogy very far, needless to say, but it accounts for what we see of destiny in tragedy, where it is the form of that which is born and dies under the same sign. And the sign which leads to life, to existence, is also the one that leads to death. It will, then, be under the same fateful sign that things begin and end. This is the meaning of that famous story of death in Samarkand ... On the town square, a soldier sees death beckoning to him. He takes fright, goes to see the king, and says, 'Death has beckoned to me; I am going to flee as far away as possible, I am fleeing to Samarkand.' The king commands that death be sent to him, to explain why it has terrified his captain. And death tells him, 'I didn't want to frighten him. I simply wanted to remind him we had an appointment tonight – in Samarkand.' So, destiny has a form which is, as it were, spherical: the further you go away from a point, the nearer you are to it.

Destiny does not, strictly speaking, have 'intentions', but you sometimes have the impression that, while a life of fame and success is taking its course, somewhere, obscurely, there is a machinery working away in the opposite direction that unforeseeably turns the euphoria to tragedy. The fateful event is not the one you can explain with causes, but the one which, at a certain moment, defies all causality, which comes from elsewhere, but with this secret destination. We may, for example, find causes for the death of Princess Diana, and attempt to reduce the event to those causes. But it is always a cop-out to appeal to causes to justify effects: we shall not exhaust the meaning or non-meaning of an event by so doing. Now, in this case, what constitutes the event is a turnabout from positive to negative, a turnabout which means that, when things are too fortunate, they turn to disaster, as though a collective sacrificial force were silently at work. Destiny is always the principle of reversibility in action. In this sense, I would say that it is the world which thinks us – not discursively, but the wrong way round, against all our efforts to think *it* the right way round. Every one of us could easily find examples of this. Even in coincidences there is a whole art. When psychoanalysis talks about slips, of word-substitutions in jokes, these things, too, are of the order of coincidence: at a particular point, there is a strange attraction between signifiers, and it is this which constitutes the psychical event.

As a counter to the completely computerized universe we are being offered or promised, I could easily imagine a world that would be nothing but coincidences. Such a world would be not a world of chance and indeterminacy, but one of destiny. All coincidences are, in a sense, predestined. Then, standing opposed to destination, to that which has a clear purpose, would be destiny or, in other words, that which has a secret destination, a pre-destination, though not in any religious sense. Predestination would say: such a moment is predestined for a particular other, such a word for another one, as in a poem where you have the impression that the words were always preordained to meet.

Similarly, in seduction, there is a form of predestination: between the feminine and the masculine I do not think there is merely a differential relation; there is also a form of destiny. The one is always destined for the other; there is an exchange, a dual form, not – contrary to the widespread conception – an individual destiny. Destiny is this symbolic exchange between us and the world, which thinks us and which we think, where this collision and collusion take place, this telescoping of, and complicity between, things.

This is where the crime lies, and the tragic dimension. Punishment arrives without fail: there will be a reversibility which will mean that something in all this will be avenged. As Canetti says: 'Where vengeance is concerned, there is no need to wish for it; it will come, it happens automatically, by the reversibility of things.' Such is the form of destiny.

IMPOSSIBLE EXCHANGE

We are in exchange, universally. All our conceptions lead back to it at some point or other, whether it be commodity exchange or that concept of symbolic exchange which I've used a great deal and which is, in a way, its opposite. The fact remains that exchange, in fact, grounds our morality, as does the idea that everything can be exchanged, that the only thing that exists is what can assume value, and hence pass from one to another.

Destiny comes close to the notion of impossible exchange, at least in the absolute. Destiny cannot be exchanged for anything. It is something which, at a particular moment, is of such singularity that it is not exchangeable against any rationality whatever. So, the radical dimension of destiny might be said to be that of impossible exchange. In my opinion, exchange is a delusion, an illusion, but everything conspires to have us act as though ideas, words, commodities, goods and individuals can be exchanged ... That death itself can be exchanged for something. And finding reasons for everything – causes and purposes – is another modality of exchange. For this delusion to function, everything has to have a referent or an equivalent somewhere. In other words, a possibility of exchange in value terms. By contrast, that which cannot be exchanged might, to cut a few corners, be said to be what Bataille terms the 'accursed share' – and this has to be reduced.

For my part, I think that, despite all our efforts, this impossible exchange is everywhere. If you take the example of the economic field, which is pre-eminently the site of exchange, everything is, in principle, exchangeable there, since that is its condition of entry to the field. But the economic sphere itself, taken overall, is not exchangeable for anything. There is no meta-economy or transcendence by which it could be measured. There is no ultimate purpose against which the economy as such could be exchanged. Within it, all forms of circulation are possible, but there isn't any kind of transcendence, any 'other thing' for which it could be exchanged as value.

And we can make this argument, more or less, about the world itself. The world is unexchangeable because, overall, it has no equivalent anywhere. Since everything is part of the world, there is nothing external against which it could be measured, to which it could be compared and hence by which it could be assessed in value terms. In a certain sense, it has no price.

But, as soon as something is named, coded, enciphered, we are back to the circuit of exchange again. At that point, the 'accursed share' becomes a value. Misfortune, misery – all these things are traded very easily these days. There is a stock exchange of negative values, so to speak. So, debt, which is something negative and at the same time something virtual, can be traded, can be bought and sold. Nietzsche, I believe, speaks of redeemed debt. This redeeming of debt is God's stratagem: he sent his son to redeem man's debt, with the effect that man will never be able to redeem it, since it has already been redeemed by the creditor. So, man will never be free of it; he will always be a debtor. And what goes for God also goes, today, for capital: the system creates an unlimited debt which it redeems as it goes along, renegotiating it and putting it back into circulation *ad infinitum* ... A bit like the devil who, having bought man's shadow, recycles it.

It is the strategy of the system itself to maintain an exchange based upon nothing, but one which has all the effectiveness of a positive exchange. The system can incorporate anything, but as such it cannot, for its part, be equivalent to anything else whatever. Any system – economic, political or aesthetic – has its internal determinants and rationale, which make exchange possible. But there is a limit, a critical mass, a demarcation line beyond which these systems no longer have any meaning, because there is nothing external to them that can ground them as value. We then enter the quasi-supernatural dimension of impossible exchange. At some point our moral law of exchange no longer operates. What are we to call this other place? It is not a universe, because the universal, according to our conception, marks out a space in which all exchanges are possible: we are in the universal of exchange. It is, at all events, a place where this reconciliation of something with its value – with the referent which gives it a meaning – can no longer be effected. So, there is no exchange any more, but a duality. Whereas in exchange, there are also two terms, but, most importantly, there is passage between them, circulation (a consensual, reconciled circulation in which the contracting parties are agreed), in this case consensus cannot operate. As a consequence, these systems are haunted by this limit, this barrier of impossible exchange. With all systems developing by an ever-increasing proliferation, saturation brings them up against this impossible-exchange barrier. And the effect of this is to throw them out of kilter internally.

But we are now in the process of inventing a fantastic general equivalent – the virtual. This presents itself as an enciphering, an encoding in which it will be possible to measure everything by the same extremely reductive yardstick: the binary, the alternation between 0 and 1. Here lies the ultimate form of exchange, its most abstract form, its limit-form, close to impossible exchange. With this idea we might associate that of uncertainty, in the sense used in the 'uncertainty principle' in physics. Everything is taking us into a world steeped in definitive uncertainty. We are no longer dealing here with that relative uncertainty that is connected with science's backwardness, or with insufficiently sophisticated mental structures. There will always be the line beyond which a system, no longer able to prove its foundedness, turns around at that point against itself. In physics the uncertainty principle states that one cannot define both the position and the velocity of a particle. For us, it signifies that one can never define both a thing – life, for example – and its price. One cannot at the same time grasp the real and its sign: we shall never again master the two simultaneously.

DUALITY

These parallel worlds are, in the end, the consequence of a reality which is coming apart because we have tried too hard to unify and homogenize it. Should we see duality – of which reversibility is, in a way, an applied form – as a principle? Might we be dealing here with an order or disorder of the world in which there would originally be two eternal principles, good and evil, coexisting antagonistically, as Manichaean thought asserts? If the created world is the work of evil, if evil is its energy, the fact that good – and truth – can be found there is quite strange. We have always wondered at the perversity of things, of human nature ... but it is the opposite question we should have asked: how can it be that, at some point, good can exist; that somewhere, in some thin layer of the world, a principle of order can be established – a principle of regulation and equilibrium that operates? Such a miracle is unintelligible.

I see things differently. What we find very difficult to understand is the dual principle, so much are we shaped by a general philosophy of unity: everything that contravenes that philosophy is deemed inadmissible. We attempt to control not that which *is*, but that which, in the name of this assumption, ought not to exist. For my part, I find it more fascinating to posit an irreversible, irreconcilable duality as the underlying principle. We set good and evil against each other in dialectical terms in such a way that a morality is possible – that is to say, in such a way that we can opt for the one or the other. Now, there is nothing to show we really have that choice, on account of a perverse reversibility which means that, most of the time, all attempts to do good produce evil in the medium or long term. And, indeed, the opposite also exists, where evil leads to good. So, there are totally contingent, totally fluctuating effects of good and evil, to the point where it is illusory to consider the two principles separately and think there is a possible choice between them based on some kind of moral reason.

To borrow the well-known metaphor of the iceberg, duality pre-supposes that good is the one-tenth of evil that protrudes above the surface ... And, from time to time, there is a turnabout: evil takes the place of good, and then the iceberg melts and everything goes back to a kind of fluid in which good and evil are merged. At any rate, I regard duality as the true source of all energy, without, however, passing any verdict on which of the two principles – good or evil – has primacy. The key thing is the antagonism between them, and the impossibility of founding a world of order and, at the same time, accounting for its total context of uncertainty. We cannot do that, and that is what evil is.

THOUGHT

The world thinks us, but it is *we* who think that . . . Thought is, in fact, a dual form; it is not the form of an individual subject, it is shared between the world and us: we cannot think the world, because somewhere it is thinking us. What we have here, then, is no longer a subject-thought, which imposes an order by situating itself outside its object, keeping that object at a distance. Perhaps that situation has never existed. Doubtless it is merely an imposing intellectual representation, though one that has gained fantastically widespread acceptance. But something has changed now: the world, appearances, the object are bursting out. The object, which we have tried to keep in a kind of analytic passivity, is taking its revenge . . . I am quite fond of the idea of this revenge, of this return-effect that forces us to take it into account. This is where uncertainty emerges, but is it thought which injects this uncertainty into the world? Or is it the radical illusion of the world that contaminates thought? This will probably be forever undecidable. The fact remains that the disappearance of the fixity of the thinking subject, the basis of our Western philosophy, and the awareness of a symbolic exchange between the world and thought are destabilizing the discourses of order and rationalization –

including scientific discourse. Thought then becomes once again a world-thought,[3] no territory of which can boast an analytical mastery of things. And if, as I think, the state of the world is paradoxical – ambiguous, uncertain, random or reversible – we have to find a thought that is itself paradoxical. If it wishes to make an impact in the world, thought must be in the world's image. Objective thought was entirely adequate for the image of a world we presumed to be determined. It is no longer so for a destabilized, uncertain world. We must, then, recover a kind of event-thought, which manages to make uncertainty a principle and impossible exchange a rule, knowing it is not exchangeable against either truth or reality. It is something else, which remains enigmatic. How can it still situate itself without claiming mastery of signification, being in the flow of appearances and not indexed to truth? This is the principle of impossible exchange, and it seems to me that thought must take this into account, must make uncertainty a rule of the game. But it must know that it is playing without any possible conclusion, in a definitive form of

3. Baudrillard glosses this notion as follows in the filmed interviews that constitute, so to speak, the audiovisual prehistory of this book: 'Et alors la pensée est remise dans le cours du monde ... elle redevient une pensée-monde, c'est-à-dire qu'elle fait événement dans le monde, mais elle est elle-même un événement du monde ... mais le monde fait événement aussi dans la pensée.' See *Mots de Passe. Jean Baudrillard* (Un film conçu par Leslie F. Grunberg, réalisé par Pierre Bourgeois), Éditions Montparnasse, 2000, video cassette 2 [Trans.].

illusion, and hence of putting-into-play[4] – including putting its own status in play.

The order of things, the order of appearances, can no longer be entrusted to some subject of knowledge or other. I want thought to be paradoxical, seductive – on condition, clearly, that seduction is not taken to mean flattering manipulation, but a *détournement* of identity, a *détournement* of being.

For thought does not work at the identification of things, like rational thought, but at their disidentification, their seduction, that is to say, their *détournement*, in spite of its phantasmatic will to unify the world under its control and in its name.

This type of thought is clearly an *agent provocateur*, managing illusion by illusion. I do not claim that it applies everywhere. Perhaps we have to accept two levels of thought: a causal, rational thought, corresponding to the Newtonian world in which we live; and another, much more radical level of thought which could be said to be part of this secret destining of the world, of which it might be a kind of fatal strategy.

4. This 'putting-into-play' reflects the etymology of the word 'illusion': in + ludere (to play) [Trans.].

THE LAST WORD

It would be extremely presumptuous to attempt to pronounce a last word. But I think we have been on a journey where the terms – death, the *fatal*, the feminine, simulation – have metabolized into one another in a kind of spiral. We have not taken a single step closer to some possible end-goal. We have merely gone through a number of paradigms that have no end other than in the moment of their metamorphosis. For if concepts die, they die a natural death, if I may put it that way, passing from one form to another – which is still the best way of thinking. So, there is no end, then; no conclusion. For me, thinking is radical in so far as it does not claim to prove itself, to verify itself in some reality or other. This does not mean that it denies the existence of that reality, that it is indifferent to its impact, but that it regards it as essential to keep itself as an element in a game whose rules it knows. The only fixed point is the undecidable and the fact that it will remain so, and the aim of the entire work of thought is to preserve that.

But the inalienable presence of that undecidable does not lead me to an unsituated thinking, concerned only with abstract speculation and with manipulating ideas from the history of philosophy. I attempt to free myself from a referential, teleological thinking precisely in order to pursue the play of a thinking which is aware that something else thinks it. This is why I have always been quite close to current events – not so much in sociological or political terms, but rather so as to measure the angle of incidence on those events of a parallel world with which a perpetual confrontation is going on.

Thought must play a catastrophic role, must be itself an element of catastrophe, of provocation, in a world that wants absolutely to cleanse everything, to exterminate death and negativity. But it must at the same time remain humanist, concerned for the human, and, to that end, recapture the reversibility of good and evil, of the human and the inhuman.